Becon

GW00866507

Christian

How you can accept Christ and grow as a new

Believer

By Karl Allen Bruss

DEDICATION

I dedicate this book to my Lord and Savior Jesus Christ. May He use it in any way that He sees fit. Also, to my wife and children, I love you. Thank you for allowing me the time to work on this book. Lastly, to my extended family, thank you for always believing in me.

Who is a Christian and how do I become a Christian?

      I say who is a Christian not what is a Christian because a Christian is a person who believes in Jesus Christ as their Savior. The word Christian has the word Christ in it and simply means that you are a follower of Jesus Christ and His teachings. To become a Christian is very simple. All you must do is accept that Jesus Christ is the Son of God, the Creator of the universe, and tell Him that you accept Him into your heart and life. Many will often say that this is it, and that is all you need to do when you become a Christian. This is not necessarily true. It is true that accepting Christ as your Savior is all you need to do to become a Christian, but it does not stop there. To be like Christ is the main goal, or at least should be the main goal of every Christian. How does a person become like Christ after they have accepted Jesus into their heart and life? It is very simple. You spend time every day talking to and praying to Him and reading His Word. It is also very important as a Christian to be baptized in water as a public confession that you are a follower of Jesus Christ. It is also very good for you as a new Christian to be around other Christians so that you can grow as a Christian by learning from seasoned Christians. It is imperative for you to pray and seek the Lord each day also. I have been a Christian for many years now and I have seen many people accept Jesus Christ into their life and then they think that is all that they need to do when they become a Christian. They do not read the Bible, God's Word and they do not, most importantly change their life. What do I mean by change their life? I mean that you were living for the devil one moment and now you are living for Jesus Christ now. This means that you should follow the teachings of Jesus Christ, not just say that you accept Him into your life and that is it. This is the hardest part for many people that were really living for the devil with all their heart. This process is called repentance. To repent of your sins means that you turn away from all the ungodly things that you were doing before you became a Christian. You were following after the devil and his ways and now you are going to follow after Jesus Christ and

His ways. To truly follow after Jesus means that you talk to Him and want to learn as much about Him as possible. This is done by praying and reading the Word of God, the Bible. It is understandable that some people accept Jesus as their Savior right before they die, and that is awesome, but you do not want to wait because you do not know if you will live until tomorrow. The Bible says that our life is just like a mist, we are here today and then we are gone tomorrow. We are not promised tomorrow, and all we have is today, this moment. You must accept Jesus Christ as your Savior and begin to study and learn as much as you can about Him. If you do not have a Bible to read, then you can get one for free at many churches. They should have some that they are willing to give out to people that are new Christians. A suggestion for you is to begin reading in the book of John in the New Testament. This is a good book for new believers to start reading and to know and grow in Jesus Christ. Tell someone that you have become a Christian and that you are a follower of Jesus Christ. This strengthens your walk with Christ as you begin to tell others about Him. Throughout the rest of this book I will tell you about the main things that you should know as a new believer in Jesus Christ. These things are very important to you as a new believer in Jesus Christ. Find a good local church that you can begin going to and let them know that you have become a Christian. If you are reading this now and want to pray and accept Jesus as your Savior, then let's pray a prayer together. Pray this right now, "Jesus, I accept you into my heart and life right now. I accept that you are the Son of God and I want to live for you now. Come into my heart and I repent of all of my sins that I have been doing. I will no longer follow after the devil and his ways; I will follow after you now Jesus Christ and your ways. In the name of Jesus, amen." If you prayed that prayer and believe it with all of your heart, you are now a Christian. Begin to live like a Christian and follow after the teachings of Jesus Christ which are found in the Word of God, the Bible. Tell others about the decision that you have just made, and you will begin to grow in Christ every day.

Salvation

Salvation, or to be saved from one's sins means that a person must believe in the Lord Jesus Christ with all their heart and accept Him into their life. Accepting Jesus as your Savior means that you understand that Jesus is the Son of God and that He died on a cross for your sins. God the Father sent His Son Jesus Christ to the earth so that we can be saved from our sins and live with Him for eternity in heaven. The alternative is to not accept Jesus into your life and to burn for eternity in hell, while being tormented by demons for all eternity. There are many scriptures that talk about salvation and we will examine many of them throughout this chapter. One of the most well-known salvation scriptures in found in **John 3:14-18 (NKJV)**, and it says, "*14 And as Moses lifted up the serpent in the wilderness, even so must the Son of Man be lifted up, 15 that whoever believes in Him should not perish but have eternal life.16 For God so loved the world that He gave His only begotten Son, that whoever believes in Him should not perish but have everlasting life. 17 For God did not send His Son into the world to condemn the world, but that the world through Him might be saved.18 He who believes in Him is not condemned; but he who does not believe is condemned already, because he has not believed in the name of the only begotten Son of God."* Jesus was hung on a cross as a punishment by the religious people of His day, in order to fulfill the plan of God. He came to the earth knowing that He would die for the sins of others. Whoever believes in Him is not condemned but has eternal life through Jesus Christ. God the Father loved the world so much that He gave us His Son Jesus Christ, so that we may believe in Him and have eternal life through Him. A few other popular salvation scriptures are found in the book of Romans. These scriptures when combined together are often called the Romans road to salvation, because they all talk about how a person can be saved by believing in Jesus Christ as their savior. **Rom. 5:8-10 (NKJV)** says, *8 "But God demonstrates His own love toward us, in that while we were still sinners, Christ died for us. 9 Much more then, having now been justified by His blood, we shall* *be saved from wrath through Him. ¹⁰ For if when we were enemies we were reconciled to God through the death of His Son, much more, having been reconciled, we shall be saved by His life."* Jesus Christ died for us while we were sinners. Jesus often dined with sinners and He loved people very much while He was on the earth. He loved us so much that He died for us so that we can be saved through Him. **Romans 6:22-23 (NKJV)** says, ²² *"But now having been set free from sin, and having become slaves of God, you have your fruit to holiness, and the end, everlasting life. ²³ For the wages of sin is death, but the gift of God is eternal life in Christ Jesus our Lord."* This portion of scripture tells us that because of sin there is death, but because of Jesus Christ, we can have eternal life. This eternal life is a gift from God the Father to us so that we can live with him for eternity. Because this is a sinful world and because we sin daily (not live a purposefully sinful life), we need an Advocate, Jesus Christ to pay the price for us so that we can be washed from our sins. The last scripture of the Romans road to salvation is found in **Romans 10:9-11 + 13 (NKJV)** and it says, "*9 that if you confess with your mouth the Lord Jesus and believe in your heart that God has raised Him from the dead, you will be saved. 10 For with the heart one believes unto righteousness, and with the mouth confession is made unto salvation. 11 For the Scripture says, "Whoever believes on Him will not be put to shame." 13 For whoever calls on the name of the Lord shall be saved."* In order for someone to be saved through Jesus Christ (the only way to be saved), one must confess with their mouth that Jesus is Lord and believe it in their heart that God the Father raised Him from the dead, then you will be saved. Whoever calls on the name of Jesus Christ shall be saved. This is how so many receive salvation right before they die. They often have glimpses of the eternal realm and understand that they must accept Jesus Christ as their Lord and Savior. The goal is to accept Him early on in your life so that you can spend the rest of your life getting to know Him better.

Philippians 2:5-11 (NKJV)

"5 Let this mind be in you which was also in Christ Jesus, 6 who, being in the form of God, did not consider it robbery to be equal with God,

7 but made Himself of no reputation, taking the form of a bondservant, and coming in the likeness of men. 8 And being found in appearance as a man, He humbled Himself and became obedient to the point of death, even the death of the cross. 9 Therefore God also has highly exalted Him and given Him the name which is above every name, 10 that at the name of Jesus every knee should bow, of those in heaven, and of those on earth, and of those under the earth, 11 and that every tongue should confess that Jesus Christ is Lord, to the glory of God the Father."

Mark 16:15-16 (NKJV)

"15 And He said to them, "Go into all the world and preach the gospel to every creature. 16 He

who believes and is baptized will be saved; but

he who does not believe will be condemned."

The Word of God

When talking about the Word of God it is clear in the Bible which is also called the Word of God, that God is the Word and that everything was made through Him in the beginning. It says in **John 1:1-5 (NKJV)** *"In the beginning was the Word, and the Word was with God, and the Word was God. 2 He was in the beginning with God. 3 All things were made through Him, and without Him nothing was made that was made. 4 In Him was life, and the life was the light of men. 5 And the light shines in the darkness, and the darkness did not comprehend it."* Many often think that when it says the Word was with

God here in this passage that it is referring to Jesus, God's Son. If this is the case, which many tend to believe, then we can simply say that Jesus is the Word of God made flesh. When Jesus came to the earth as a baby through the virgin Mary, conceived of the Holy Spirit, Jesus became the Word of God made into flesh. Jesus' goal while He was on the earth was to do the will of the Father, His Father. Since Jesus came to the earth to only do the will of the Father, then it is safe to say that if we follow the teachings and the words of Jesus, then we will also be fulfilling the will of the Father. Throughout the Bible, especially in the New Testament, because the New Testament was literally being written as it was taking place, many people quote from the Old Testament, even Jesus Himself. Jesus often told those who were listening to Him speak in the temple when He was reading from the scrolls of the Old Testament, He said, the Word of God is fulfilled in your hearing today. Wow. To be that bold in front of the people listening, to say that He was fulfilling the prophesies from the Old Testament, He was often telling those listening that He was equating Himself with God the Father. This is the very reason that many wanted to kill Him. Even satan, the tempter came to Jesus and quoted the scriptures in **Mathew 4:3-10 (NKJV)** it says, [3] *"Now when the tempter came to Him, he said, "If You are the Son of God, command that these stones become bread." [4] But He answered and said, "It is written, 'Man shall not live by bread alone, but by every word that proceeds from the mouth of*

God.' " [5] Then the devil took Him up into the holy city, set Him on the pinnacle of the temple, [6] and said to Him, "If You are the Son of God, throw Yourself down. For it is written: 'He shall give His angels charge over you,' and, 'In their hands they shall bear you up, Lest you dash your foot against a stone.' " [7] Jesus said to him, "It is written again, 'You shall not tempt the LORD your God.' " [8] Again, the devil took Him up on an exceedingly high mountain, and showed Him all the kingdoms of the world and their glory. [9] And he said to Him, "All these things I will give You if You will fall down and worship me." [10] Then Jesus said to him, "Away with you, Satan! For it is written, 'You shall worship the LORD your God, and Him only you shall serve.'" As we can see from the scripture, even satan knows the scriptures. Knowing the scriptures alone does not mean that you will go to heaven, or even that you truly know Jesus and God the Father. Spending time in prayer, meditating on the Word of God and talking with Jesus like He is your friend and brother is how you will truly get to know Him and have a relationship with Him. It also says in **Luke 5:5 (NKJV),** *"So it was, as the multitude pressed about Him to hear the word of God, that He stood by the Lake of Gennesaret".* When Jesus taught the crowds of people, he most often told them modern day parables that the people could relate to. He often used parables that had to do with farming, fishing, and other regular daily activities. Jesus spoke the Truth to the people, and they knew that He spoke the very words from God. Signs and wonders followed Him wherever He went confirming the Word. The next scripture is one of these parables that He spoke about. The parable of the different soils which represents our hearts and the seeds that are sown onto these different types of soils which represent the Word of God. It says in **Luke 8:11 (NKJV),** [11] "*Now the parable is this: The seed is the word of God.* [12] *Those by the wayside are the ones who hear; then the devil comes and takes away the word out of their hearts, lest they should believe and be saved.*" So, based on this parable from Jesus, the Word of God can be heard but not received in the heart. The goal is to hear the Word of God and have good fertile soil which the seed of the Word falls on and produces a great crop (fruit). This fruit that is from the sowing of the Word of God is lasting fruit and will grow well in a heart that is ready to receive the Word. You have to pray before reading the Word of God or before hearing someone preaching the Word of God, that your heart is ready to receive the seed of the Word that you are about to read or hear. This heart that is ready to receive the seed of the Word is the heart that God is looking for in all of us. If you have not already prayed before reading this, then you can stop right now and pray that the Word of God that is written in this book that you are reading will fall on the fertile soil of your heart so that you can produce fruit for the Kingdom of God. Another great scripture about the Word of God that is similar to the words from the parable of the soils is **Luke 11:28 (NKJV),** *28 "But He said, "More than that,* *blessed are those who hear the word of God and keep it!"* Jesus says that you are blessed when you hear the Word of God and are able to keep it. As you remember from the parable of the soils, Jesus said that satan will try to come and take the seed away from you so you will not produce any fruit for the Kingdom of God. Any time you are ready to hear or read the Word of God, prepare your heart for the Word to take root and grow so that you can bear fruit. How do you bear fruit from hearing and reading the Word of God? Well, you do what it says. You tell others about the Word of God and about the life of Jesus, God's Son, and then you are producing fruit that lasts. You also produce fruit by having and demonstrating the fruits of the Spirit. The fruits of the Spirit are mentioned in **Galatians**

chapter 5 and are: love, joy, peace, patients, kindness, goodness, self-control, faithfulness, and gentleness. Demonstrating these fruits of the Spirit in your life will allow people to ask you, what is different about you, or something is different about you, what is it? Then you can share with them the good news of the gospel of Jesus Christ. I want to share a few more great scriptures with you about the Word of God:

Ephesians 6:17-18 (NKJV)

[17] "And take the helmet of salvation, and the sword of the Spirit, which is the word of God; [18] praying always with all prayer and supplication in the Spirit, being watchful…"

Hebrews 4:12 (NKJV)

"For the word of God is living and powerful, and sharper than any two-edged sword, piercing even to the division of soul and spirit, and of joints and marrow, and is a discerner of the thoughts and intents of the heart."

Revelation 22:18-19 (NKJV)

18 " For I testify to everyone who hears the words of the prophecy of this book: If anyone adds to these things, God will add to him the plagues that are written in this book; 19 and if anyone takes away from the words of the book of this prophecy, God shall take away his part from the Book of Life, from the holy city, and from the things which are written in this book."

Luke 4:16-22 (NKJV)

¹⁶ "So He came to Nazareth, where He had been brought up. And as His custom was, He went into the synagogue on the Sabbath day, and stood up to read. ¹⁷ And He was handed the book of the prophet Isaiah. And when He had opened the book, He found the place where it was written:

¹⁸ "The Spirit of the Lord is upon Me,
Because He has anointed Me
To preach the gospel to the poor;
He has sent Me to heal the brokenhearted,
To proclaim liberty to the captives
And recovery of sight to the blind,
To set at liberty those who are oppressed;
¹⁹ To proclaim the acceptable year of the Lord."

²⁰ Then He closed the book and gave it back to the attendant and sat down. And the eyes of all who were in the synagogue were fixed on Him. ²¹ And He began to say to them, "Today this Scripture is fulfilled in your hearing." ²² So all bore witness to Him and marveled at the gracious words which proceeded out of His mouth. And they said, "Is this not Joseph's son?"

Baptism (in water and in the Holy Spirit)

What is baptism according to the Word of God? When Jesus was baptized by his cousin John, he went down to the Jordan river to be baptized by him. John was baptizing people into the Kingdom of God, but when people asked him if he was the Messiah he said, *" I am the voice of one crying in the wilderness: "Make straight the way of the LORD""* **(John 1:23 NKJV)** John was fulfilling the scriptures that the prophet Isaiah said about him. John was sent to make way for Jesus and to prepare people's hearts to hear the message of Jesus Christ. Jesus came to John to be baptized also, and John said in **John 1:29**

(NKJV), "*Behold! The Lamb of God who takes away the sin of the world!*" The Bible goes on to say in **Matthew 3:16 (NKJV),** [16] "*When He had been baptized, Jesus came up immediately from the water; and behold, the heavens were opened to Him, and He saw the Spirit of God descending like a dove and alighting upon Him.*" As a Christian, we must follow after the example of our Savior Jesus and also be baptized. Jesus tells His disciples in **Matthew 28:19 (NKJV),** "*[19] Go therefore and make disciples of all the nations, baptizing them in the name of the Father and of the Son and of the Holy Spirit.*" This is a command from Jesus for us today. Not only must we go and make disciples and share the good news of Jesus with others, He wants us to also be baptized in the name of the Father, the Son, and the Holy Spirit. Jesus also tells us that since He went away to be with His Father in heaven, that He would send The Advocate, The Holy Spirit to be with us and to live inside us. The Holy Spirit will fill you when you call out to Him and ask Him to fill you. This is a different experience from your salvation experience. When you become a Christian, you accept that Jesus is the Lord of your life, but you need the power of the Holy Spirit to walk through this life today. We know that being baptized with water is different from being baptized with the Holy Spirit. These two things are different according to the scriptures. It says in **John 1:32-34 (NKJV),**

"**32** *And John bore witness, saying, "I saw the Spirit descending from heaven like a dove, and He remained upon Him. **33** I did not know Him,* *but He who sent me to baptize with water said to me, 'Upon whom you see the Spirit descending, and remaining on Him, this is He who baptizes with the Holy Spirit.' ³⁴ And I have seen and testified that this is the Son of God."* John said that he baptized with water but there is one who will baptize with the Holy Spirit and that is Jesus. So just to be clear, you become a Christian by accepting Jesus into your heart and life. You get baptized in water to show the world that you are now a follower of Jesus Christ and then there is also another experience you have as a Christian called being filled with the Holy Spirit. Jesus is our example of this as it says in the scriptures, Jesus was baptized then the Holy Spirit came upon him. It also says in **Luke 4:1 (NKJV)**, *"Then Jesus, being filled with the Holy Spirit,* *returned from the Jordan and was led by the Spirit into the wilderness."* Clearly it states that Jesus was filled with the Holy Spirit before He was led into the wilderness to be tempted by the devil. We should know that this is a separate experience from being baptized with water. The thing is though, many times when people are baptized with water, the Holy Spirit comes upon them when they come up out of the water like Jesus, and they are filled with the Holy Spirit and start speaking in the Holy Spirit, which is often called speaking in tongues. What do I mean by speaking in tongues? Well the scriptures tell us that speaking in the Holy Spirit or speaking in tongues is a promise from God. It says in **Acts 1:4-5 (NKJV)**, 4 *"And being assembled together with them, He commanded them not to depart* *from Jerusalem, but to wait for the Promise of the Father, "which,* He said, *"you have heard from Me;* ⁵ *for John truly baptized with water, but you shall be baptized with the Holy Spirit not many days from now."* The disciples went and prayed and waited to be filled with the Holy Spirit as promised by Jesus. It happened to be the day of the festival of Pentecost when they were all gathered together praying and it says in **Acts 2:2-4 (NKJV),** ² *"And suddenly there came a sound from heaven, as of a rushing mighty wind, and it filled the whole house where they were sitting.* ³ *Then there appeared to them divided tongues, as of fire, and one sat upon each of them.* ⁴ *And they were all filled with the Holy Spirit and began to speak with other tongues, as the Spirit gave them utterance."* As we can see from the scriptures to be baptized with water is a command given to us by Jesus and then we pray for and wait for the Holy Spirit to come upon us as we walk out our lives as Christians. Today, we need the power of the Holy Spirit to be upon us like never before. I will not get into the debate of whether speaking in tongues is evidence of being filled with the Holy Spirit, but I will say that from personal experience, when I speak in the Holy Spirit I feel His presence, help, comfort, guidance, and His hand upon me like I did not feel when I was not praying and speaking in the Holy Spirit. As you know, it is not all about our feelings, but to know that the Holy Spirit is working inside you because you feel His presence and guidance upon you, then there is no denying it, you need the Holy Spirit to come upon you to help you throughout your life. You can be filled with the Holy Spirit right now. Pray with me, "Holy Spirit, come and fill me, I need you." Wait for Him to fill you and continue to pray for Him to fill you. Do not give up, keep asking. He will come and fill you and you will feel His power come upon you and you can share your experience with someone else. Tell others about what God has done for you, and you will begin to see Him move in power through you like never before. Submit to His will and He will use you like you never even imagined. The scriptures go on to say in **Acts 2:38 (NKJV)** "38 *Then Peter said to them, "Repent, and let every one of you be baptized in the name of Jesus Christ for the remission of sins; and you shall receive the gift of the Holy Spirit."* So, Peter mentions something else here that we as Christians must walk in and live in, and it is called repentance. Peter tells the people to repent and accept Jesus as their Lord and savior, then the Holy Spirit will come upon them. So, there is a process that you must follow when you become a Christian. You must repent of your sins, ask Jesus to come into your life, then you are baptized in water and you pray for the Holy Spirit to come upon you and fill you. Many times, when the Holy Spirit comes upon you will feel something welling up within your belly, and you will want to speak out and pray out in the Holy Spirit. It is ok. Let Him have control and you will feel His power upon your life to witness and share the good news of Jesus Christ with others.

Prayer

Praying is very important for you as a new Christian. Learning to pray every day to our Heavenly Father is so very important for us. Prayer is when you talk to the Heavenly Father and Jesus in an intimate way. You have to first understand that Jesus is near to you, and that He hears you when you talk to Him. This is what prayer is, you are sharing your heart with Jesus and the Father. The more that you learn to share your heart with Jesus here on the earth, the closer that I believe you will be able to be with him when you enter into eternal life with Him. As a Christian, it should be your goal now to get as close to Jesus as you can while you are here on the earth so that when you get to heaven, you will truly know Jesus and who He is. This can only be done by spending time with Him and getting to know Him in an intimate way. This is done by just simply talking to Him in prayer and reading His Word the Bible. Prayer is all throughout the Bible, so I will choose some of my favorite scriptures regarding prayer and the importance of prayer, for us to look at in the Old and New Testament.

In the Old Testament people prayed to God the Father, often in a time of need. God the Father would dwell in the temple that the people would set up with specific directions from the LORD. Many times, the priest would go into the house of the LORD and seek after God's heart for the people, then they would come out and tell the message of the LORD to the people. In **I Kings 8:27-29 (NKJV)** it says, *27 "But will God indeed dwell on the earth? Behold, heaven and the heaven of heavens cannot contain You. How much less this temple which I have built! 28 Yet regard the prayer of Your servant and his supplication, O LORD my God, and listen to the cry and the prayer which Your servant is praying before You today: 29 that Your eyes may be open toward this temple night and day, toward the place of which You said, 'My name shall be there,' that You may hear the prayer which Your servant makes toward this place."* The Creator of the world told the people that He would come down and dwell among them, as they cried out to Him in prayer. We have to take note here of the language used when it says prayer and supplication. Here it is saying that we need to be talking with God and making requests known to God with a passionate heart. We need to take this example and use it today in our lives when we pray. Prayer is not just asking God for things, it is a part of prayer, but we need to seek his face and not just his hand. We need to truly try to get to know Him as a person would get to know another person, but with a passionate heart.

The Bible also says in **II Chronicles 7:1-3 (NKJV)** *"When Solomon had finished praying, fire came down from heaven and consumed the burnt offering and the sacrifices; and the glory of the LORD filled the temple. ² And the priests could not enter the house of the LORD, because the*

glory of the LORD had filled the LORD's house.
[3] When all the children of Israel saw how the fire
came down, and the glory of the LORD on the
temple, they bowed their faces to the ground on
the pavement, and worshiped and praised
the LORD, saying: "For He is good, For His mercy
endures forever." The first notable thing here
that happened is that fire from heaven come
down and consumed the offering. So, based on
this we know that there is fire in heaven that has
a purpose. It says it consumed the burnt offering.
It was already burnt by fire, but it was not
consumed by heavenly fire. We can take note
today that we as Christians need to have
ourselves consumed with the fire from heaven
and not just with the things or "fire" from earth.
We should constantly seek the will of heaven

and the fire from heaven for our lives. The second notable thing happening here in these verses is that after the fire from heaven consumed the sacrifice, the glory of the LORD filled the temple. The application for us today is that when the fire from heaven consumes us, we can be filled with his glory and we will feel His presence. If we could only know a fraction of what is being talked about here, I believe that we could truly walk in His presence here on the earth daily. We just need to be an acceptable sacrifice to the Lord, and He will consume us with HIs fire. The next portion states that the people, when they saw the fire from heaven and the presence of the LORD, they bowed down and worshiped and praised Him. We also need to do this today. We need to make a habit of bowing down to worship and praise the Lord and we know that His fire will come and consume us. The last part of the verses says that His mercy endures forever. This tells us that today we can experience the mercy of the Lord just like they did in the days of the Old Testament. We need the mercy of the Lord, and we need to cry out for his mercy each day for us, our family members, and for our nation.

The next scripture that I chose about prayer is from **Ezra 10:1 (NKJV)** and it says, *"Now while Ezra was praying, and while he was confessing, weeping, and bowing down before the house of God, a very large assembly of men, women, and children gathered to him from Israel; for the people wept very bitterly."* This is such a powerful verse about prayer. It tells us that while talking to God we should confess our sins, weep before Him, and bow down before him. These three things are very much needed in our lives today. We need to humble ourselves before the Creator of the universe, bow down, and confess and weep before Him often. I believe that when we do this He hears from heaven and responds. He always hears our prayers, but there is quite a difference in the "way" that we pray. We need to be humble before our Lord. Confession of sins is another great thing that we need to do daily. The Bible says in **John 1:9 (NKJV)** *"If we confess our sins, He is faithful and just to forgive us our sins and to cleanse us from all unrighteousness."* Make confession of your sins a daily part of your prayer life with Jesus and your relationship with

Him will continue to grow and grow. You will start to realize that you are actually confessing a lot less things to Him as you grow in Him because you are living a righteous life before Him.

As we continue into the New Testament, there are many prayers and passages on prayer, but I want to just share a few of my favorites with you that I think will help you grow in your faith in Jesus Christ as a new believer in Him. It says in **Mark 11:24-26 (NKJV)** *24 "Therefore I say to you, whatever things you ask when you pray, believe that you receive them, and you will have them 25 "And whenever you stand praying, if you have anything against anyone, forgive him, that your Father in heaven may also forgive you your trespasses. 26 But if you do not forgive, neither will your Father in heaven forgive* *your trespasses."* There are two great and powerful truths we must realize. The first one is that when you pray you have to believe that your prayers are being heard and answered right then. Sometimes it takes a while for the actual answer to reach you and your situation because there is a fight in the heavenly realms for you and your soul. The demons and satan want to hinder you and your prayers any way that they can. They will go to war instantly to try to hinder your prayers from happening. It is your job to just believe that He hears your prayers and will answer them in His timing. The second thing that is powerful in this passage is the fact that you must forgive others so that your prayers will not be hindered. We must walk through our day with a heart of forgiveness towards others. When, not if, someone offends you throughout your day, you need to instantly forgive them and move on with your day. Holding bitterness and unforgiveness in your heart will hinder your walk with God. I agree that it is hard sometimes to forgive quickly, but it must be a goal of yours each and every day. Forgiveness is a great key to having unhindered prayers.

The next portion of scripture is one of my favorites because this is when the disciples ask Jesus to teach them how to pray. The passage is found in **Luke 11:1-4 (NKJV)** and it says, *"Now it came to pass, as He was praying in a certain place, when He ceased, that one of His disciples said to Him, "Lord, teach us to pray, as John also taught his disciples." 2 So He said to them, "When you pray, say: Our Father in* *heaven, hallowed be Your name. Your kingdom come your will be done on earth as it is in heaven. [3] Give us day by day our daily bread. [4] And forgive us our sins, for we also forgive everyone who is indebted to us. And do not lead us into temptation but deliver us from the evil one."* There are so many great things here that we can learn from Jesus about prayer. The first thing we need to realize is that Jesus had a place that He liked to go to pray to His Father. He set aside a time and a place to talk to His Father. We need to make a point to do the same thing in our daily lives. I wake up early in the morning to pray because I want to start out my new day right. I want to bathe my day in prayer before the sun even comes up in the morning. There have been so many times throughout my life where I stood and said to the sun, I have risen up before you again to seek the Son. Jesus goes on to tell His disciples what to pray by saying, "when you pray say…" and this should be a key for us that we need to also pray this way because Jesus taught His disciples that this is the way that they should pray. One of the main things that stands out in His teaching about how to pray is when He says, "Your will be done on earth as it is in heaven". This is such a powerful thing to tell the Lord, that you want His will to be done in your life, not your will to be done. I pray this prayer each and every morning of my life in the morning, and I believe that when I start my day by saying that I want His will to be done in my life, He hears from heaven and acts on my behalf. He knows that I want His will to be done in my life because I tell Him that I only want what He wants for my life. I only want to do His will each and every day. If you start your day praying and believing this in your heart, you have started your day out right. Lastly, He talks about forgiveness again. It is so important to forgive others. I believe that we do not even realize how important forgiveness really is in our lives. Live your day out forgiving others like Jesus did. Some of Jesus' last words while He was on the cross was a prayer to His Father to forgive the people that were hurting Him, and that they really did not know what they were doing. Forgive others when they hurt you and your Heavenly Father will bless you.

The next portion of scripture talks about people gathering together to pray. It is found in

Acts 12:12 (NKJV) and it says, [12] *"So, when he had considered this, he came to the house of Mary, the mother of John whose surname was Mark, where many were gathered together praying."* I have included this passage to show you that it is not only very important to spend time praying by yourself each and every day, but it is also so important to pray with other believers as well. It says that many were gathered together praying. It is important for us to realize, that there is power in prayer with other believers. The Bible also says in **Mathew 18:20 (NKJV)**, *"For where two or three are gathered together in My name, I am there in the midst of them."* When we gather together in the name of Jesus with other believers, He shows up. This is very important for us to realize. It also says in the previous verse in **Mathew 18:19 (NKJV)** that, *19 "Again I say to you that if two of you agree on earth concerning anything that they ask, it will be done for them by My Father in heaven."* It states here again that there is power when you pray with other believers. He says that if we agree concerning "anything" it will be done. This is hard to grasp for so many people, I think. It says anything we ask when we agree, will be done by our Father in heaven.

Another powerful scripture about prayer is found in **Acts 16:25-26 (NKJV)** and it says, *25 "But at midnight Paul and Silas were praying and singing hymns to God, and the prisoners were listening to them. 26 Suddenly there was a great earthquake, so that the foundations of the prison were shaken; and immediately all the* *doors were opened, and everyone's chains were loosed."* This scripture shows us that there is power in prayer. When Paul and Silas were in prison they should have felt down and out according to the standards of the world. Instead, they began to pray and change the atmosphere around them. When you pray and seek the will of the Father, He hears you. When they were praying and singing out in the prison, they changed their circumstances. There was a great earthquake, and everyone had the opportunity to go free if they wanted, but no one left. Why did no one leave? I believe that God had a greater purpose here. After the Jailor saw that no one had left, he asked Paul how to be saved, and his whole household was saved.

My hope and prayer for you is that you will understand the importance of prayer in your life today. You need to rise early and pray to the Father in Jesus name each and every day. He is a rewarder of those who diligently seek Him the Bible says. Seek Him each and every day in prayer as you find your place that you call your special prayer place, and do not forget to gather together with other believers to pray as well. There is power in the prayers of agreement. Remember, where two or more are gathered, He is there with you. Here is a great prayer from David:

Psalm 17:3-9 (NKJV)

"3 You have tested my heart; You have visited me in the night; you have tried me and have found nothing; I have purposed that my mouth

shall not transgress. [4] Concerning the works of men, by the word of Your lips, I have kept away from the paths of the destroyer. [5] Uphold my steps in Your paths, that my footsteps may not slip. [6] I have called upon You, for You will hear me, O God; incline Your ear to me, and hear my speech. [7] Show Your marvelous lovingkindness by Your right hand, O You who save those who trust in You from those who rise up against them. [8] Keep me as the apple of Your eye; hide me under the shadow of Your wings, [9] From the wicked who oppress me, from my deadly enemies who surround me."

The Blood of Jesus

When we talk about the blood of Jesus, it is important to know and realize how important that the shedding of His blood really was, and how important it is for us today. Without the blood of Jesus, we would not have forgiveness for our sins. The Bible says in **Mathew 27:26b-31 (NKJV)**, "*26b When he had scourged Jesus, he delivered Him to be crucified. 27 Then the soldiers of the governor took Jesus into the Praetorium and gathered the whole garrison around Him. 28 And they stripped Him and put a scarlet robe on Him. 29 When they had twisted a crown of thorns, they put it on His head, and a* *reed in His right hand. And they bowed the knee before Him and mocked Him, saying, "Hail, King of the Jews!"* [30] *Then they spat on Him, and took the reed and struck Him on the head.* [31] *And when they had mocked Him, they took the robe off Him, put His own clothes on Him, and led Him away to be crucified."* This is talking about Jesus Christ the Savior of the world, God the Father's Son. They beat Him by whipping Him and punching Him in the face, hit Him with a rod, put a crown of thorns on His head, and spit on him, all before they led Him to be crucified. I believe this may be why they found someone along the way to help Jesus carry the cross to the place of His crucifixion. Once there, the soldiers nailed him to a wooden post, or cross, and He suffered there for many hours, taking upon Himself the sins of the world so that we can be forgiven. This is why the Bible says that God His Father turned away from Him, in verse 46 of chapter 27, it says, *"My God, My God, why have You forsaken Me?"* Where God the Father is, there is no sin. Jesus did all of this for you and me. He died and bled for you and me so that we may be forgiven of our sins and live with Him for eternity in heaven. **Rom. 5:8-10 (NKJV)** says, *"8 But God demonstrates His own love toward us, in that while we were still sinners, Christ died for us. 9 Much more then, having now been justified by His blood, we shall be saved from wrath through Him. 10 For if when we were enemies we were reconciled to God through the death of His Son, much more, having been reconciled, we shall be saved by*

His life." God the Father loved us so much that He provided a way for us to be forgiven and to be reconciled with Him. While we were still sinners, He sent His Son and He died for us. He knows all and He knows that you will need forgiveness for your sins, so over 2000 years ago He died and shed His blood so that you can be forgiven today. When we accept Him as our Lord and Savior, He cleanses us with His blood, and we are forgiven of our sins. Asking forgiveness for our sins is a daily process, and as you grow in Him you will need to ask Him for forgiveness for things less and less. As we continue to grow in Him and read His Word, we should be living a life that is separate from the rest of the world. If someone is not a follower of Christ, they are an enemy of God, even though

He loves all and wants all to come to Him. God the Father provided a way for us to be forgiven, and it is only through the blood of Jesus Christ His Son. There is no other way to go to the Father except through the blood of Jesus Christ. Many religions throughout the world try to say there are many different ways that you can get to heaven or get to the Father God, but these all are false religions. Again, there is only one way to be forgiven of sins and that is through the blood of Jesus. It also says in **I Peter 1:18-20 (NKJV)** that, "*18 knowing that you were not redeemed with corruptible things, like silver or gold, from your aimless conduct received by tradition from your fathers, 19 but with the precious blood of Christ, as of a lamb without blemish and without spot. 20 He indeed was* *foreordained before the foundation of the world but was manifest in these last times for you."* Simply put, we need the blood of Jesus, the blood of the Lamb who was slain, the precious blood of Jesus to wash our sins away so that we can stand before him blameless and with no spots or blemishes on ourselves. Where God is, there is no sin and the blood of Jesus takes away and washes away all of our sins, if we confess them to Him. It also says in **I John 1:7 (NKJV)** *"But if we walk in the light as He is in the light, we have fellowship with one another, and the blood of Jesus Christ His Son cleanses us from all sin."* To walk in the Light of Jesus means that our goal is to be like Him. He is our Master and if we want to follow after the Light, Jesus, then we need the blood of Jesus to cleanse us from all of our sin. There is no one that has no sin. There are just those of us who are Christians who strive to be like our Master Christ, and to do that we walk through our day trying our best through the Holy Spirit to flee from all sin. He helps us, and when we do screw up and sin, He is faithful and just and forgives us of our sin and cleanses us from all unrighteousness. In **Revelation 12:11-12 (NKJV)** it says, *"11They overcame him by the blood of the Lamb and by the word of their testimony, and they did not love their lives to the death. 12 Therefore rejoice, O heavens, and you who dwell in them! Woe to the inhabitants of the earth and the sea! For the devil has come down to you, having great wrath, because he knows that he has a short time."* We have to realize that we have overcome satan and demons by the blood of the Lamb. After we accept Him as our Savior, we ask Him for forgiveness, and He cleanses us from all unrighteousness because He shed His blood for us.

Repentance

The message of repentance is not a popular message in churches today, and I think that many people do not even know what repentance is. What does it mean to repent? Repentance means, to turn away from sin and dedicate yourself to God. You could be living a sinful life and doing sinful things, but when you hear the message of repentance and you turn the other direction and confess your sins to Jesus and accept Him into your life, you are saved.

To turn from sin means that you were going this way towards the things of the world, then you repent and ask God for forgiveness of your sins, then you start going the other way, towards the things of God. It is a total change of mind, heart, and actions. There are many scriptures throughout the Bible that have to do with repentance. If you have never been serving God, if you are turning back to God and you have fallen away from Him, you can repent today and start following after Him.

Jesus is talking with the religious leaders of the day again and He tells them and the multitudes of people there with Him in **Matthew 3:7 (NKJV)** *"8 Therefore bear fruits worthy of repentance".* Jesus continually spoke against the religious leaders of the day because they were supposed to be leaders of the people, and they were often called "Brood of Vipers" by Jesus.

John also knew that they were just for show and acted "religious" and did not repent from their evil ways. He warned them over and over again to repent, and their eyes were blinded to the truth. As Christians today we are to demonstrate the power of God by healing the sick, raising the dead, and casting out demons, then the people will know that the kingdom of heaven is at hand. There are signs that are following them that believe today. Where the kingdom of heaven is, there is no sickness and there is no death. Many men and women of God around the world are preaching this message of repentance and are seeing the signs that follow just like Jesus said would happen. The message of repentance: John the Baptist preached it, Jesus preached it, Peter preached it, Paul preached it, and we should preach it. We must discern the signs of the times. Jesus is coming soon. Today there are the rapid acceleration of events in history that tell us that our time here on the earth may be short. Sure, even my grandmother said that, her mother would say that Jesus was coming back real soon when she was a child, and that was back in the early 1900's.

Jesus was in a solitary place praying and his disciples came to him and said everyone is looking for you. Jesus said, *"Let us go somewhere else to the nearby villages so that I can preach there also. That is why I have come." So, he traveled throughout Galilee, preaching in their synagogues, and driving out demons.* **Mark 1: 36-39 (NKJV)**

Jesus says, I am coming back soon. I am coming back for a spotless bride. Revelation says that He will come like a thief in the night and no one will know the day or the hour that He will come, and that we are to be ready and to be watchful. You must turn from evil and stop sinning. Jesus will not come back for people that keep on sinning. We must repent! Repentance is not just something that you just do one time either, when you get your life right with Christ. Repentance is a continual and ongoing thing that we must do to cleans ourselves with the blood of Jesus. We must realize the urgency of the hour! Will you be ready?

This is not a popular message with many people. It is easy to be comfortable and continue to live in a life of sin. I believe that satan will not bother you if you are not a threat to his kingdom. The demons should say when you wake up, "Oh no he is awake what can we do to stop him today." Do the demons in hell know who you are, or will they say, like the demons in **Acts 19:15 (NKJV)** *"the evil spirit answered and said, "Jesus I know, and Paul I know; but who are you?"* Jesus is coming back soon, and we must tell others the good news of Jesus. If we do not tell others about the message of Jesus, then I believe we are being disobedient to what Jesus told us to do. Remember, Jesus said, "As you GO…say this, the kingdom of heaven is near". We should not be afraid of what people say or think of us because we are doing what Jesus told us to do. Jesus says in **Matthew 10:22 (NKJV),** 22 *"And you will be hated by all for*

My name's sake. But he who endures to the end will be saved." Verse 24 also says that a student is not above his teacher or a servant above his master. They persecuted Jesus and I believe that if we stand for righteousness we will also be persecuted for our faith. Jesus says in **Matthew 24:14 (NKJV),** *14 "And this gospel of the kingdom will be preached in all the world as a witness to all the nations, and then the end will come."* What an awesome verse. The gospel cannot go to the ends of the earth if we are still sitting in the pews of the church! We must go out and tell others that He is coming soon.

God says in **Revelation 3:15-16, (NKJV)** *15 "I know your works, that you are neither cold nor hot. I could wish you were cold or hot. 16 So then, because you are lukewarm, and neither* *cold nor hot, I will vomit you out of My mouth."*

This is quite a scripture to ponder. He says that you should either be hot or cold not lukewarm. He will spit/vomit you out of His mouth if you are just living a lukewarm life. Either follow after God or do not. The time is coming shortly when a sword will fall separating the hot and the cold and there will not be any that will be lukewarm, in the middle. I call these kind of people "fence riders". Those who try to get as close to the world as they can and still go to church on Easter and Christmas or even on Sundays, and then go on and live like the devil during the week. These type of people God says are lukewarm and He will soon spit/vomit you out of His mouth. Please heed my warning and the warning of others today. Choose you this day whom you will serve. Will you serve the devil, or will you serve the Creator of the universe? You must choose this day. We are not promised another minute here on the earth. Our life is like a mist. The Bible says in **James 4:14 (NKJV)** "*For what is your life? It is even a vapor that appears for a little time and then vanishes away.*" Just like a spray of water in the air, our life is just a brief and short time then it just goes away. Many have said that they will just wait until the last minute to accept Jesus and just choose to live their life however they want to. This is playing with fire. The fires of hell are knocking right at your door if you are thinking or acting like this.

You can accept Jesus Christ right now if you do not know him, or you can rekindle the fire you once had within you. You can pray this prayer with me and believe it with all your heart and you will be saved. "Jesus, I believe that you are the Son of God, and that you died for me on a cross. You rose again on the third day and are now seated at the right hand of the Father, our Father. I accept you into my heart and life Jesus Christ, and I will choose to follow after you all the days of my life. I love you Jesus and I accept you as the Lord of my life. In your name Jesus, Amen." If you prayed that prayer, please contact one of your local pastors and tell him or her that you accepted/rededicated your life to Jesus Christ and you would like to talk with them about it. They will make time to talk with you about the things of God and help you grow in Him. Surround yourself with other believers in the

Faith to help build up your faith in Him. Your local pastor can also talk with you about being baptized. If you are now a believer in Jesus Christ, you can go and tell others about what Jesus Christ has done for you. You can tell others about the Good News of Jesus Christ and that they must repent of their sins like you did today. May God our Father truly bless you with every spiritual blessing.

ABOUT THE AUTHOR

It is the heart of the author that this book somehow finds its way to you and that you will accept Jesus Christ as your Savior. Karl attended Southwestern Assemblies of God University where he completed his undergraduate studies in Church Ministry and later went on to complete his M.Ed. at SAGU also. He has taught in public schools, private schools, and in Christian schools in America and abroad. Karl and his family have visited and lived in several different countries. They like to hike and experience the outdoors together as a family and share their experiences with others. They look forward to sharing many more adventures together.

Printed in Great Britain
by Amazon